# BIG BEASTS
# Giraffe

Stephanie Turnbull

SAUNDERS BOOK COMPANY

Published by Saunders Book Company
27 Stewart Road, Collingwood, ON Canada L9Y 4M7

U.S. publication copyright © 2013 Smart Apple Media.
International copyright reserved in all countries.
No part of this book may be reproduced in any form
without written permission from the publisher.

Created by Appleseed Editions, Ltd.
Designed by Hel James
Edited by Mary-Jane Wilkins

Library of Congress Cataloging-in-Publication Data

Turnbull, Stephanie.
  Giraffe / Steph Turnbull.
       p. cm. --  (Big beasts)
  Includes index.
  Summary: "An introduction on giraffes, the big beasts in African grasslands. Describes how giraffes move, find food, communicate, and care for their young"--Provided by publisher.
  ISBN 978-1-77092-118-4 (pbk)
  1. Giraffe--Juvenile literature.  I. Title.
  QL737.U56T87 2013
  599.638--dc23
                                   2012004113

Photo acknowledgements
l = left, r = right, t = top, b = bottom
page 1 pandapaw/Shutterstock; 3 iStockphoto/Thinkstock;
4 Doug Vinez/Shutterstock; 5 iStockphoto/Thinkstock;
6 J Reineke/Shutterstock; 7 Riaan van den Berg/Shutterstock;
8 javarman/Shutterstock; 9 Anup Shah/Thinkstock;
10-11 iStockphoto/Thinkstock; 12 iStockphoto/Thinkstock;
13t iStockphoto/Thinkstock, b Peter Betts/Shutterstock;
14 Hemera/Thinkstock; 15 Theodore Mattas/Shutterstock;
16 Hemera/Thinkstock; 17 Mogens Trolle/Shuttterstock;
18 iStockphoto/Thinkstock; 19 Jeff Grabert/Shutterstock;
20 ecliptic blue/Shutterstock, 21 Andrejs Jegorovs/Shutterstock;
22 Vishnevskiy Vasily/Shutterstock; 23l iStockphoto/Thinkstock;
r karamysh/Shutterstock
Cover PeterMooij/Shutterstock

Printed in the United States of America,
at Corporate Graphics in North Mankato, Minnesota.
DAD0503
042012
9 8 7 6 5 4 3 2 1

# Contents

Hello Up There!   4

Spotty Fur   6

Finding Food   8

Munch, Munch   10

Difficult Drinking   12

On the Lookout   14

Watch Out!   16

Big Babies   18

Growing Up   20

BIG Facts   22

Useful Words   24

Index   24

Giraffes are **huge!**

# Hello Up There!

Giraffes are the tallest animals in the world.

They tower over other animals on the African grasslands.

Giraffes have the same number of bones in their neck as you do ... just much **LONGER!**

# Spotty Fur

Giraffe fur is covered in browny-red blotches. No two giraffes have exactly the same pattern.

They have two furry horns.

Birds called oxpeckers help giraffes by eating insects in their fur.

# Finding Food

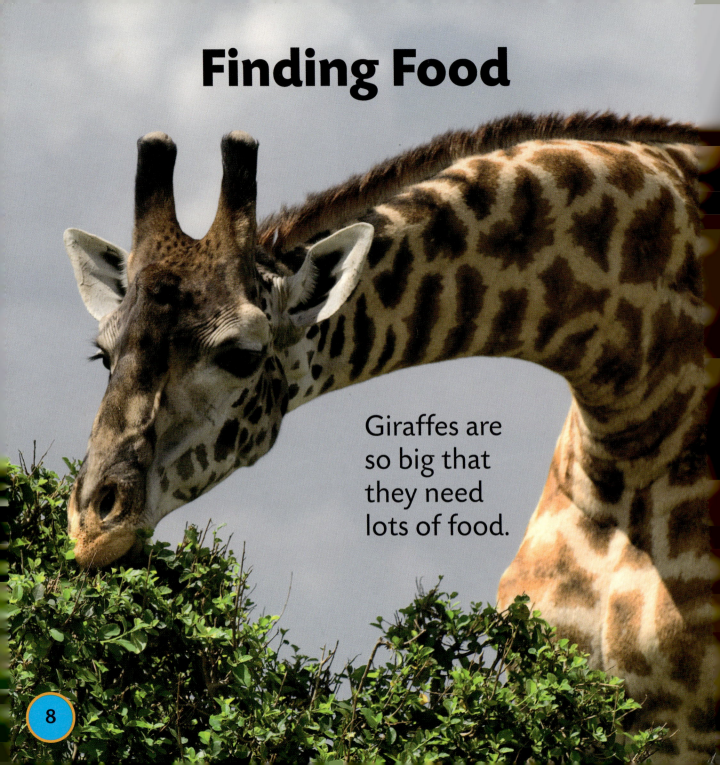

Giraffes are so big that they need lots of food.

All day they search for tasty leaves. Their favorite trees are called acacias.

They can **s t r e - e - e t c h** up to leaves that other animals can't reach.

# Munch, Munch

**Giraffes have an extra-long tongue to grab twigs and pull off leaves.**

They swallow everything, then bring it back up later to chew properly.

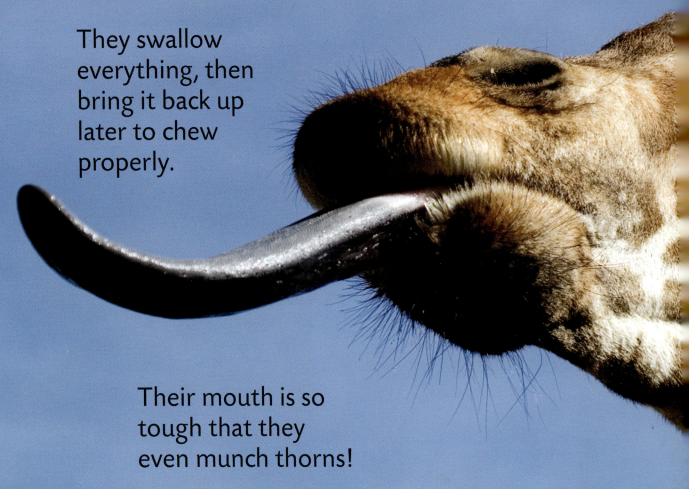

Their mouth is so tough that they even munch thorns!

# Difficult Drinking

Drinking is tricky for giraffes. They spread their front legs and lean forward awkwardly.

Lions or crocodiles might attack giraffes as they drink, so other giraffes stand guard.

# On the Lookout

Giraffes stand most of the time to watch for lions. They can even sleep standing up.

They see a long way!

If they spot a lion, they gallop away before it gets close.

# Watch Out!

Giraffes are gentle but strong. One powerful **KICK** can kill a lion.

Sometimes male giraffes swing their necks like hammers to **thwack** each other. Fights don't last long, and usually no one is hurt.

# Big Babies

Giraffe babies are called calves.

Mothers have their baby standing up. The calf hits the ground with a BUMP!

Calves stand before they are an hour old, and run soon after.

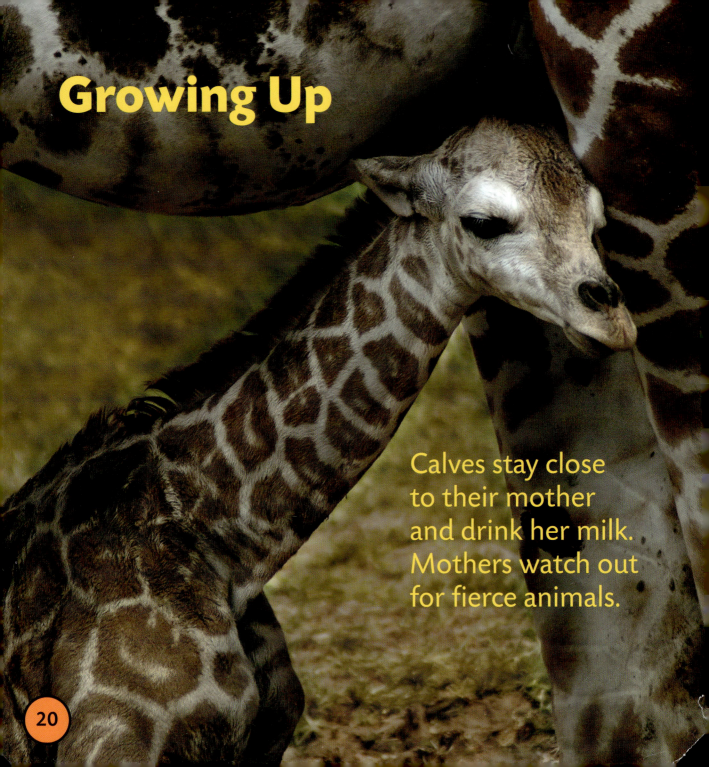

# Growing Up

Calves stay close to their mother and drink her milk. Mothers watch out for fierce animals.

When calves are older, they join other young giraffes. One mom babysits while the others find food.

Calves chase each other, bump noses and have play fights.

# BIG Facts

Giraffes are taller than you and three friends standing on each other's shoulders.

Newborn calves are taller than an adult human.

Giraffes have hooves the size of dinner plates and a tongue as long as your arm.

A giraffe could peer in your bedroom window!

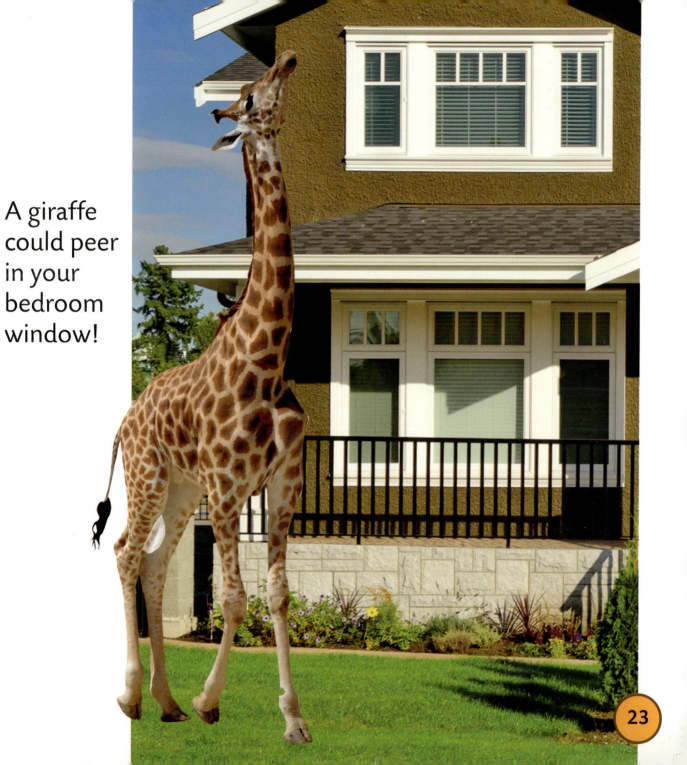

## Useful Words

**calf**
A baby giraffe.

**hoof**
A giraffe's big, hard foot. Giraffes kick lions with their hooves.

**horn**
A hard bump on a giraffe's head. All giraffes have horns.

**grassland**
A large, open, grassy area.

## Index

calves  18, 19, 20, 21, 22

fighting  16, 17, 21
food  8, 9, 10, 21
fur  6, 7

horns  6
hooves  22

legs  12

neck  5, 16, 17

tongue  10, 22

## Web Link

Go to this website for great giraffe facts and videos:
www.bbc.co.uk/nature/life/Giraffe